# F I R E  F L I E S

Published by Smart Apple Media

123 South Broad Street

Mankato, Minnesota 56001


Copyright © 1999 Smart Apple Media.

International copyright reserved in all countries.

No part of this book may be reproduced in any form

without written permission from the publisher.

Printed in the United States of America.


Photos: J. E. Lloyd, Univ. Florida

Design &Production: EvansDay Design

Project management: Odyssey Books


Library of Congress Cataloging-in-Publication Data

Halfmann, Janet, 1944-

Fireflies / Janet Halfmann. - 1st ed.

p.  cm. – (Bugs)

Includes bibliographical references and index.

Summary: describes the habitat, life cycle, behavior,

predators, and unique characteristics of fireflies.

ISBN 1-887068-33-3 (alk. paper)

1. Fireflies–Juvenile literature.  [1. Fireflies.]  I. Title.

II. Series: bugs (Mankato, Minn.)

QL596.L28H375  1998

595.76'44–dc21                    98-15364


First Edition   9 8 7 6 5 4 3 2

# FIREFLIES

Janet Halfmann

PHOTOGRAPHS BY JAMES E. LLOYD

O N A WARM SUMMER EVENING JUST AFTER SUNSET, A TINY LIGHT *flashes* IN THE DARKNESS. SOON IT IS JOINED BY ANOTHER *flashing* LIGHT, AND ANOTHER. THE TINY LIGHTS *blink* ON AND OFF. SOME LIGHTS TWINKLE IN THE AIR AND OTHERS FROM THE GROUND. IT'S A *magic light show!* THE FLASHING LIGHTS COME FROM FIREFLIES. THEY HAVE BEEN MAKING *light* AND CAPTIVATING CHIL-DREN AND ADULTS AROUND THE WORLD FOR HUNDREDS OF YEARS. WHAT ARE THESE TINY LIVING FLASHLIGHTS, AND

*why are they flashing?*

# The Firefly's Family

The firefly has "fly" in its name, but it is not a true fly. The clue is the firefly's two pairs of wings. True flies have only one pair.

Fireflies belong to the ORDER, or group, of insects called beetles. There are more SPECIES, or kinds, of beetles than any other insect. Almost half of the world's insects are beetles.

*Fireflies like this one are beetles. Most kinds of fireflies give off light, but not all of them.*

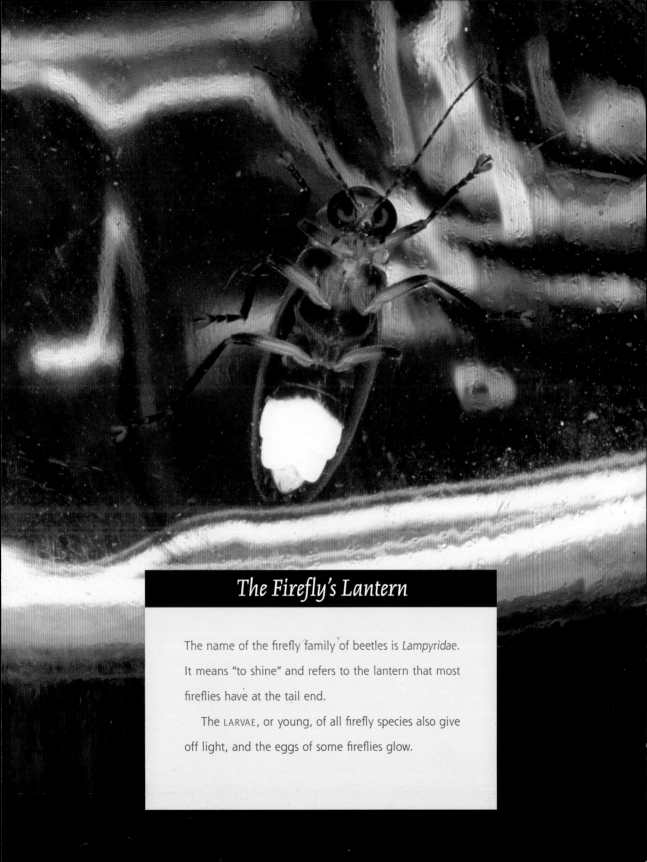

## The Firefly's Lantern

The name of the firefly family of beetles is *Lampyridae*. It means "to shine" and refers to the lantern that most fireflies have at the tail end.

The LARVAE, or young, of all firefly species also give off light, and the eggs of some fireflies glow.

# Habitat

Just about anywhere you live, you can find fireflies. There are over 2,000 species of fireflies in the world. They live on every continent except Antarctica.

About 170 species live in the United States and Canada. Most live east of the Rocky Mountains because fireflies like moist grassy or wooded areas. The most common firefly genera in eastern North America are named *Photinus* and *Photuris*.

You can find fireflies along the edges of woods, in marshes, near streams and

*Fireflies like moist, natural areas away from city lights.*

The light of this Photinus pallens *male from Jamaica is so bright that it's like a flashbulb going off.*

ponds, in fields and meadows, in the park, and in backyards. They like moist, natural areas away from city lights.

Fireflies especially like tropical climates found in Southeast Asia, Latin America, and the Caribbean Islands. That's where you'll find fireflies with the most brilliant lights, such as the Jamaican *Photinus pallens.*

If you get too close, its light is blinding, like a flashbulb going off.

***Also Called Lightning Bugs*** In North America, fireflies are often called lightning bugs. That's because most North American species flash their lights on and off like lightning. *Photinus, Photuris,* and

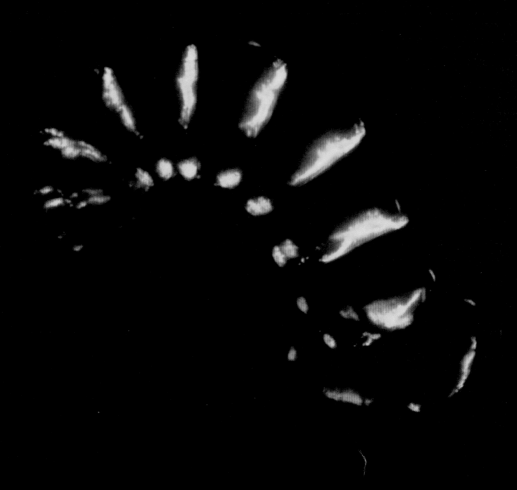

many other fireflies put on this evening light show from June to August.

Some species of fireflies give off a steady glow instead of flashing. One such firefly is the common glowworm *(Lampyris noctiluca)* of Europe. Only the wingless female gives off light. She waits, brightly glowing, until the male notices her with his keen eyes. In the United States, the female wingless pink glowworm (*Microphotus angustus*) has a steady glow. This pinkish firefly lives in California, Oregon, and Colorado.

A few kinds of fireflies don't give off light at all or have a very weak light. They are sometimes called "fireless" fireflies. For example, most fireflies west of the Rocky Mountains, such as *Ellychnia*, are fireless fireflies. Some fireless fireflies such as *Pyropyga*, live in both the western and eastern United States.

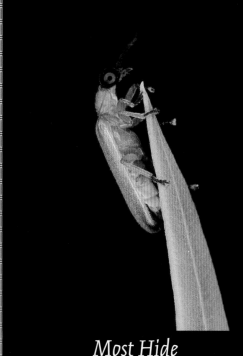

## Most Hide During the Day

During the day, you won't see most fireflies. Only the fireless fireflies are active in daylight. The night-lighting fireflies hide during the day in leafy branches, under bark, in grass, or beneath stones.

But at sunset, male night-lighters climb to the top of leaves and take off into the sky. Females climb to the top of blades of grass where they can twist and turn to show off their light.

*This glow is from the lights on the back and sides of a female giant glowworm beetle. She's a relative of the firefly.*

# Body and Senses

Like all insects, the firefly has a tough outer covering called an EXOSKELETON, which gives it support and protection. That means it has no bones inside its body. Also, like all insects, the firefly has six legs and breathes air. Its body has three parts: head, thorax, and abdomen.

***Narrow Head*** The firefly's narrow head has two eyes, two antennae, and a mouth. Its eyes are large and can see in many directions at once. The male especially can see very well, so he can spot the female's flash in the grass below as he flies through the sky. Two ANTENNAE, or feelers, stick out of the firefly's head. They help it smell, feel, and hear. The firefly's mouth has chewing jaws, like most beetles.

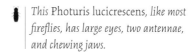

*This Photuris lucicrescens, like most fireflies, has large eyes, two antennae, and chewing jaws.*

***Thorax Is the Middle*** The THORAX, or chest, of the firefly supports its six legs and two pairs of wings. A shield at the front of the thorax covers most of the firefly's head and often has colorful markings.

Most fireflies, like most beetles, have two pairs of wings. The front wings are actually wing covers. These wing covers fold over and protect the back wings, which are used for flying.

These special wing covers give beetles their group name, *Coleoptera*, meaning "sheath wings." A SHEATH is a protective case or cover.

*The firefly's wing covers protect flying wings beneath. This male* Photinus consimilis *often hovers as he flashes.*

Male fireflies are the fliers. Females fly very little or not at all. Some females have short wings or are wingless.

***Abdomen Is Home of Light***   The firefly's ABDOMEN, or last section, is where the light action is. The insect's light organ, called a LANTERN, is on the underside of its abdomen at its tail end. It looks yellow even when it is not lit.

The abdomen also contains the heart, digestive system, and reproductive organs.

## Ordinary in Daylight

Fireflies are slender, flat, and .2 to 1 inch (5 to 25 mm) long. Females are often larger than males, as in many groups of insects. The female needs room to carry her eggs.

Fireflies look ordinary in daylight. That's good for them because they blend in with their surroundings, so it's harder for birds and other enemies to see them. Most fireflies are dull brown or black with a bit of red, orange, or yellow. But when night comes, most fireflies turn on the light magic!

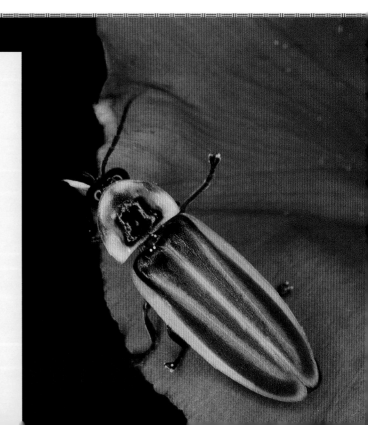

# The Firefly's Light

The firefly's lantern contains two light-making substances, luciferin and luciferase. Both names come from the Latin word *lucifer*, which means "to bring light."

The light-making substances shine when mixed with oxygen from the air and ATP, the main energy source of all living cells. ATP provides the energy necessary for the firefly's light to be produced, just as it provides the

energy for all life processes, such as jumping and blinking. The firefly can control turning the light on and off.

***Many Creatures Glow*** Light made by living things is called BIOLUMINESCENCE. An amazing number of creatures glow. Most of them live in the sea where they use their light to find their way and to attract mates and prey. There you

*You can see the lantern of this male* Photuris pennsylvanica *on the underside of his abdomen at the tail end.*

will find the angler fish dangling a light to lure prey and the lantern fish with many lights, even on its tongue.

Some other insects also glow. The large click beetle (*Pyrophorus noctilucus*) of tropical America is one of the brightest of all. Two large green lights on its back glow like bright headlights, and another light shines on its underside. Four click beetles give enough light to read a book!

Another amazing beetle light-maker is the railroad worm (*Phrixothrix tiemanni*) of South America. It has 11 pairs of green lights on its sides and red headlights! It looks like a tiny passenger train chugging along.

---

*Cool Light*   The light made by fireflies and other living things is cool. If you touch a firefly's light, you won't feel any heat at all. That's because when a firefly makes light, hardly any of the energy is wasted as heat. The firefly's glow gives off almost 100 percent light and less than 1 percent heat. In contrast, a lightbulb gives off only 10 percent light and a whopping 90 percent heat. Just think how bright a lightbulb would be if it were powered by fireflies!

People used insect light long before electricity. Chinese scholars studied by firefly light, and people living in jungles put fireflies in their hair to give light.

*These glowing ribbons were made by the pair of lights on a* Pyrophorus *click beetle as it walked from place to place.*

*Mating Lights*    Fireflies use their lights to find mates in the dark. Most do it by flashing messages. Each kind of firefly has its own special blinking code. That's important because a firefly can mate only with a firefly of its own species.

Most of this light "talking" takes place on warm

summer evenings, starting at sunset. The male flies through the air, flashing his bright light on and off in a regular pattern. Below, a female perches on a blade of grass looking for the right signal from her species of firefly.

When the female sees the appropriate signal, she waits and then flashes back. She has to pause just the right amount of time or her answer won't be right. The male sees her flash and flies closer. Again he flashes his code, and she answers. They repeat their signals until they find each other and mate.

Firefly codes are surprisingly complex. They vary depending upon the brightness of the light, how long it stays on or off, and the number of flashes. Also, the various species flash at different times of the night and fly at different heights.

*These male and female* Pteroptyx valida *have found one another on a bush in Thailand.*

*This* Photinus marginellus *firefly can be seen flashing near bushes.*

***J Shape in the Sky*** If you look carefully at the flashing lights, you can pick out different kinds of fireflies.

One of the most familiar species east of the Rocky Mountains is *Photinus pyralis.* The male starts flashing his yellow light at sunset. He flies close to the grass, dipping up and down. Every six seconds he flashes, just as he swoops upward from a dip. His long flash makes a glowing J shape in the air. The female waits two seconds, then answers with a single long flash.

The light of another common male firefly *(Photuris versicolor)* can be seen in the treetops. This firefly flashes a bright green light from early evening to midnight. He flashes quickly three to five times, pauses two seconds, then flashes his signal again. The female answers with one flash.

*Photinus marginellus* flashes from the

bushes, *Pyractomena angulata* has an orange light that flickers 8 to 10 times in a row, and *Photinus consimilis* hovers as he flashes.

You might try imitating some of the signals with a flashlight. Who knows, a firefly might "talk" to your flashlight!

---

**Blinking Tree**    Some male fireflies team up. Along riverbanks in Southeast Asia, thousands of males named *Pteroptyx* have been gathering for years in trees along riverbanks. They all flash together at exactly the same time. They create giant blinking trees, and they attract lots of females—and tourists.

North America has a team light show, too, in Texas, Florida, and North Carolina. In North Carolina, the show is put on by the firefly *Photuris frontalis*.

*This Photuris frontalis firefly teams up with other males to flash on and off all together.*

## Tricky Females

Many male fireflies in North America have to be on the lookout for a group of tricky females named *Photuris*. They imitate the signals of other females, such as *Photinus*. The tricky females hope to attract a *Photinus* male—to eat! The queen of these tricksters is *Photuris versicolor*. She can imitate 11 different species.

Scientists recently learned that *Photuris* females are after more than a good meal. They want the defensive chemicals that *Photinus* fireflies have, but that they lack. The *Photuris* need the chemicals to keep spiders, birds, and bats from eating them and the eggs they will lay.

# Life of the Firefly

The firefly's life, like that of most insects, has four stages: egg, larva, pupa, and adult. This process of growth is called METAMORPHOSIS, which means "change of form."

***Glowing Eggs*** The female firefly lays up to 100 eggs in moist places on or in the ground. As each egg comes from her abdomen, it is united with male sperm that has been stored in her body since mating. Now the female firefly's job is done. She dies a few days later. The male most likely has already died.

The tiny round eggs of most fireflies glow with a soft light. They are no bigger

*These eggs were laid by a glowworm firefly in the Appalachian Mountains in Maryland.*

*The firefly larva looks like a wiggly worm and has two lights near its tail.*

than the tip of a pencil. The eggs are left all alone, but almost all of them will hatch.

---

*Larva with Lights*   Up to a month later, a tiny brown LARVA, or young firefly, bites its way out of the egg. It looks like a wiggly worm. Two tiny lights shine near its tail. The baby is called a GLOWWORM because of its light. Often wingless female adults are also called glowworms.

The larva has one main job: to eat a lot so it will grow. It hides until night, and then wriggles above or under the ground looking for food. It likes slugs, earthworms, and especially snails. How can a tiny glowworm capture a snail five times its size? Easy. It poisons the snail with its bite. The poison turns the snail's insides to a soft liquid that is easy to eat. (Don't worry, the larva doesn't bite people.)

The larvae of some Asian species live in water. They search for food at the water's bottom, breathing through tube-like gills on the abdomen.

With all this eating, the larva's skin gets too tight. Soon it splits its skin and wiggles out of it. A new larger skin is underneath. This process is called MOLTING. All insects molt several times.

The firefly larva eats during warm weather and sleeps during cold weather.

This process can take two years for a larva that lives on land, as most do. For a larva that lives in water, it takes one year. In spring, when the larva is full grown, it prepares for a big change.

***Pupa–Big Change***   The larva of most species makes a dirt room for itself above or below the ground. Then it settles down to rest. Within two weeks, it sheds its skin for the last time. A hard, see-through shell

*Most kinds of fireflies go through the pupal stage in a dirt room above or below the ground. But the pupa of the* Pyractomena borealis *shown here hangs from a tree trunk.*

*This* Pyractomena borealis *firefly is white because it has just emerged from its pupa. In a few hours, it will darken.*

forms over its body. It is now a PUPA.

Inside, lots of changes are taking place.

Wings, longer antennae, longer legs,

larger eyes, and a new light are forming.

After two to three weeks, the change is

complete. The shell of the pupa splits

and the adult firefly pushes its way out.

It no longer looks anything like a larva.

In a few days, it will chew its way out of the dirt room. It will be ready to find a mate.

**Short Adult Life**   The firefly has reached the last stage of its life. It will live only 5 to 30 days. During this short time, it has an important job to do. It must find a mate, so new baby fireflies can grow up and flash their lights for all to see.

## Firefly Meals

Since adult fireflies live such a short time, most of them don't eat at all. They live on fat that they stored up during their time as larvae. Some may feed on nectar or pollen from flowers. An exception is *Photuris*. The female *Photuris* tricks and eats male fireflies of other species. Some *Photuris* prey on insects other than fireflies. For example, a Mexican species of *Photuris* preys on mosquitoes and beetles. Fireflies also drink water and dew from plants.

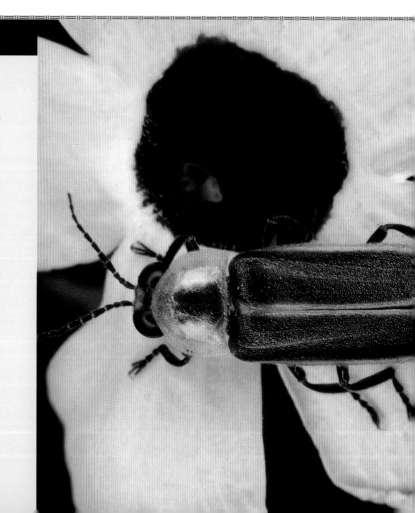

# Firefly Enemies

The firefly's growth from egg to twinkling adult is a long and dangerous journey.

First, the eggs can't get too dry, or they won't hatch. Then, both larvae and adults have to watch out for animals that like to eat them. Scientists have found that the larvae's glow warns enemies that they taste bad, but sometimes they get eaten anyway. Birds, toads, spiders, and especially frogs like fireflies. Frogs sometimes eat so many that they glow!

Perhaps the firefly's worst enemies are

*Many animals, such as this spider, catch and eat fireflies.*

human beings. Insecticides used to kill insect pests in fields, gardens, and lawns can kill fireflies as well. Fireflies have also lost habitat, as wetlands, fields, and forests have been replaced by shopping malls and residential developments. Bright city lights, too, keep fireflies away. Fireflies do best in clean, natural, dark environments.

*Fireflies like this one depend on us to protect the places where they live.*

# Fireflies and Us

The twinkling of fireflies adds beauty and magic to our lives. Many would say that is more than enough.

But the firefly does much more! Farmers and gardeners have long loved fireflies. The larvae eat slugs and other pests from the soil, but never nibble on plants. Fireflies don't bite, sting, or burn, either.

We can thank the firefly for giving us the idea for products using chemical light. This cool light, similar to that of the firefly, shines in lightsticks, rope necklaces, disposable flashlights, and emergency lights of all kinds. Cool light is especially useful because it cannot cause fire or an explosion.

*Lighting Up Science*   The uses of firefly light keep growing. For example, scientists are using firefly light to find out quickly what medicines work to treat tuberculosis. Scientists light up the tuberculosis bacteria with firefly light, then apply the medicine. If the bacteria stop glowing, they have been killed and the medicine works!

Firefly light may even signal life on other planets, such as Mars. Scien-

tists can mix Martian soil with all of the things needed to make firefly light, leaving out one key ingredient: ATP, which is the energy source of all life. If the soil lights up, scientists know that ATP exists in the soil and therefore there is the possibility of life.

Fireflies have been talking to each other with their light for hundreds of years, and now they are talking to us, too. Their light show is truly magic!

*This scientist is displaying a tube of chemical light like a glowing mushroom in the forest. He wants to see if flies are attracted to the light at night to lay eggs.*

## BOOKS

*Fireflies*, Caroline Arnold, Scholastic Inc., 1994

*Fireflies*, Sylvia A. Johnson, Lerner Publications Company, 1986

*Fireflies*, Bernice Kohn, Prentice-Hall, 1966

*Fireflies*, Joanne Ryder, Harper & Row, 1977

*The Firefly*, Yajima Minoru, Raintree Publishers, 1986

*Flash, the Life Story of a Firefly*, Louise Dyer Harris and Norman Dyer Harris, Little, Brown and Company, 1966

*Living Light: Exploring Bioluminescence*, Peg Horsburgh, Julian Messner, 1978

*Nature's Living Lights: Fireflies and Other Bioluminescent Creatures*, Alvin and Virginia Silverstein, Little, Brown and Company, 1988

*Suburban Wildlife*, "Fireflies, the Animated Lanterns," Richard Headstrom, Prentice-Hall, 1984

## FIELD GUIDES

*A Field Guide to the Beetles of North America*, Richard E. White, sponsored by the National Audubon Society, 1983

*How to Know the Beetles*, Ross H. Arnett, Jr., 1980

*Introduction to North American Beetles*, Dr. Charles S. Papp, 1984

*National Audubon Society Field Guide to North American Insects & Spiders*, 1995

*Simon & Schuster's Guide to Insects*, Ross H. Arnett, Jr. and Richard L. Jacques, Jr., 1981

## WEB

"Add a Little Spark to Your Summer Nights," Dr. Bug feature article (F. Tom Turpin, Purdue University)

"Bioluminescence," College Lecture—Light Production and Its Role in Communication in Fireflies, P. J. Albert, Department of Biology, Concordia University, Montreal, Canada

"Fireflies Flash to Electrify Mates," Tom Ellis, Michigan State University

"Glow, Little Glow Worm—Lightning Bug," Tom Ellis, Michigan State University

"Glowing Research," *Science News*, September 20, 1994

"On Colorado Fireflies," CSU Coop Extension Pest Alert Bulletin, Vol. 13, No. 11, July 5, 1996

"Summer Science: Firefly Babies Advertise Their Bitter Taste, UD Researchers Say," interview with Douglas W. Tallamy, University of Delaware

"TB Test Uses Firefly Glow," *Science News*, May 19, 1993

"What Gives Lightning Bugs the Ability to 'Glow'?" The Mad Scientist Network, question answered by Kelleen Flaherty, biology/invertebrate zoology expert

## ENCYCLOPEDIAS AND REFERENCE BOOKS

*Compton's*, 1989

*Encyclopedia Americana*, 1995

*Encyclopedia Britannica*, 1993

*Grolier* online

*The Illustrated Encyclopedia of Wildlife*, 1991

*The Marshall Cavendish International Wildlife Encyclopedia*, 1988

*The World Book*, 1996

## MAGAZINE ARTICLES

"Glowing Talk," Susan J. Tweit, *Cricket*, July 1993, pp. 11+

"Lighting up the Lab," *Harvard Health Letter*, January 1994, p. 8

"Wing-borne Lamps of the Summer Night," Paul A. Zahl, *National Geographic*, July 1962, pp. 48+

## MUSEUMS

California Academy of Sciences
Golden Gate Park
San Francisco, CA

The Milwaukee Public Museum
Milwaukee, WI

Natural History Museum of
Los Angeles County
Los Angeles, CA

Smithsonian Institution
Washington, DC

# INDEX

**A**
abdomen 12, 14, 22, 24
angler fish 16
antennae (feelers) 12–13, 25
ATP 15, 30

**B**
beetles 6
bioluminescence 9–11, 15–19, 23, 29–30
  luciferase 15
  luciferin 15
  scientific uses of 30

**C**
click beetle (*Pyrophorus noctilucus*) 16
*Coleoptera* ("sheath wings") 13
communication 17–19

**D**
diet 23–24, 26, 29

**E**
eggs 7, 22–23, 27
enemies 27–28
exoskeleton 12
eyes 12, 25

**F**
family
  *Lampyridae* 7
fireless fireflies 11

**G**
genera
  *Ellychnia* 11
  *Photinus* 8, 9, 20

*Photuris* 8, 9, 26
*Pteroptyx* 20
*Pyropyga* 11
giant glowworm beetle 10
glowworm 10, 11, 22, 23

**H**
habitat 8–11, 20, 24, 26, 28
head 12

**L**
lantern 7, 14, 15
lantern fish 16
larva (glowworm) 7, 22, 23–25, 27
legs 12, 25
life span 22
luciferase 15
luciferin 15

**M**
mating 17–19, 22
metamorphosis 22
molting 24
mouth 12

**P**
pupa 22, 24–25

**R**
railroad worm (*Phrixothrix tiemanni*) 16

**S**
sexual dimorphism
  females 10–11, 14, 18–19, 22, 23, 26
  males 11, 12–14, 18–19, 22, 26
sheath 13

species 6
  common glowworm (*Lampyris noctiluca*) 10
  *Photinus consimilis* 20
  *Photinus marginellus* 19
  *Photinus pallens* 9
  *Photinus pyralis* 19
  *Photuris frontalis* 20
  *Photuris versicolor* 19, 21
  pink glowworm (*Microphotus angustus*) 10–11
  *Pteroptyx valida* 18
  *Pyractomena angulata* 20
  *Pyractomena borealis* 24

**T**
thorax (chest) 12, 13

**W**
wings 6, 13